JUST MARRIED COLORING BOOK

CRYSTAL
COLORING BOOKS

ISBN-13: 978-1986301657
ISBN-10: 1986301656

A
Good Marriage
Is Where You Both
Think You Got The
Better
Deal

My Wife Is
Dressed To Kill
Her Face Looks
The Same Way!

I
Always Hold
Her Hand While
Out
If i Let Go She
Shops

The
Way To Get
A Husband
To Remember
Your Anniversary
Get Married On
His B'Day

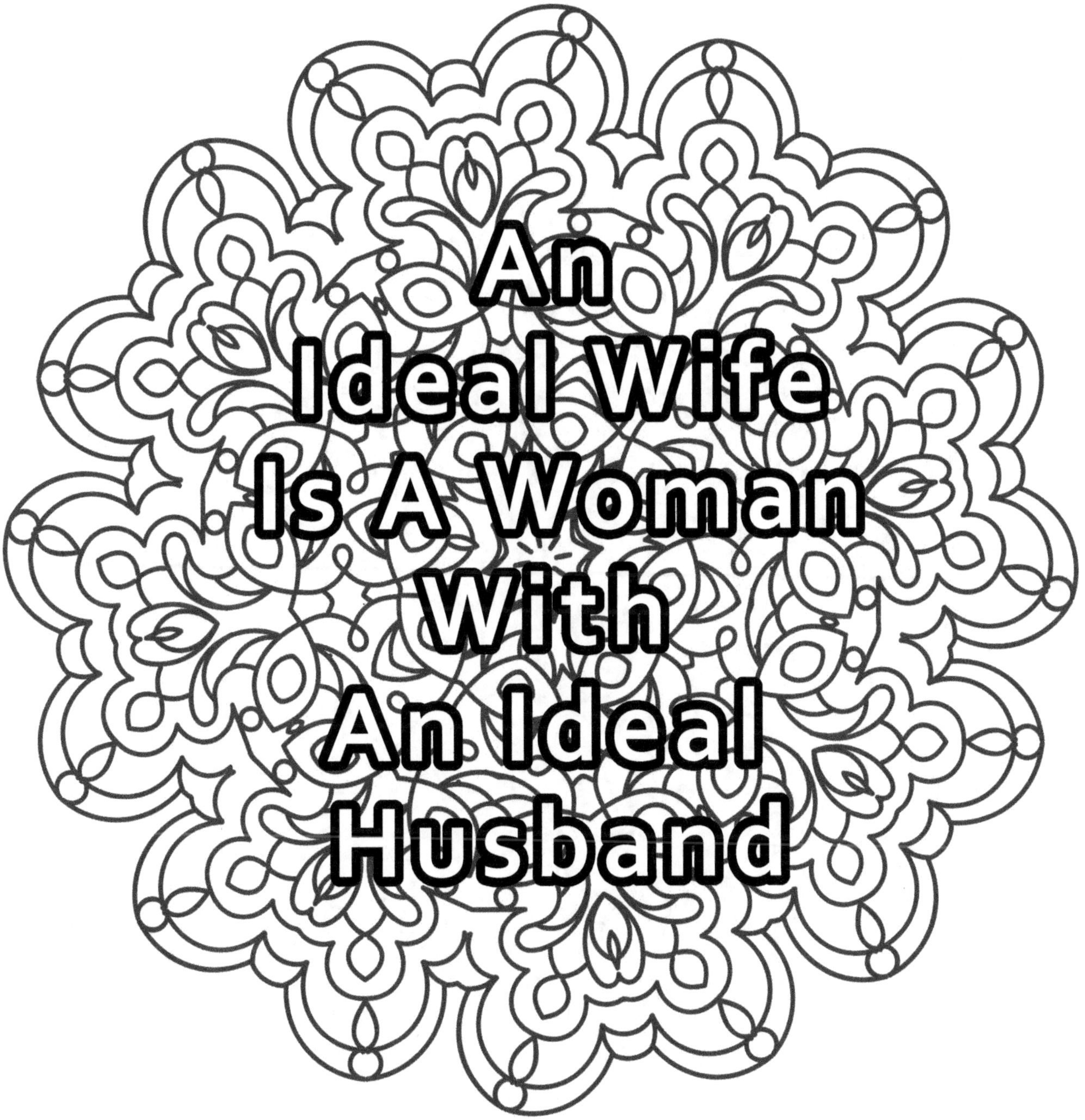
An
Ideal Wife
Is A Woman
With
An Ideal
Husband

I
Love You
no Matter What
You Do ...
But Do You Have
To Do So Much
Of
It?

Behind
Every
Sucessful
Man
Is A Sucessful
Woman

There
Are Only Three
Things A Wife
Needs
Food Water And
Compliments

How
To Get Your
Husband To Do
Anything...
Tell Him He is
Too Old
ToDo
It

When
You Are Wrong
Admit It ...
If You Are
Right
Shut Up

A
Name For
A Man That Is
Wrong About
Everything...
The
Husband

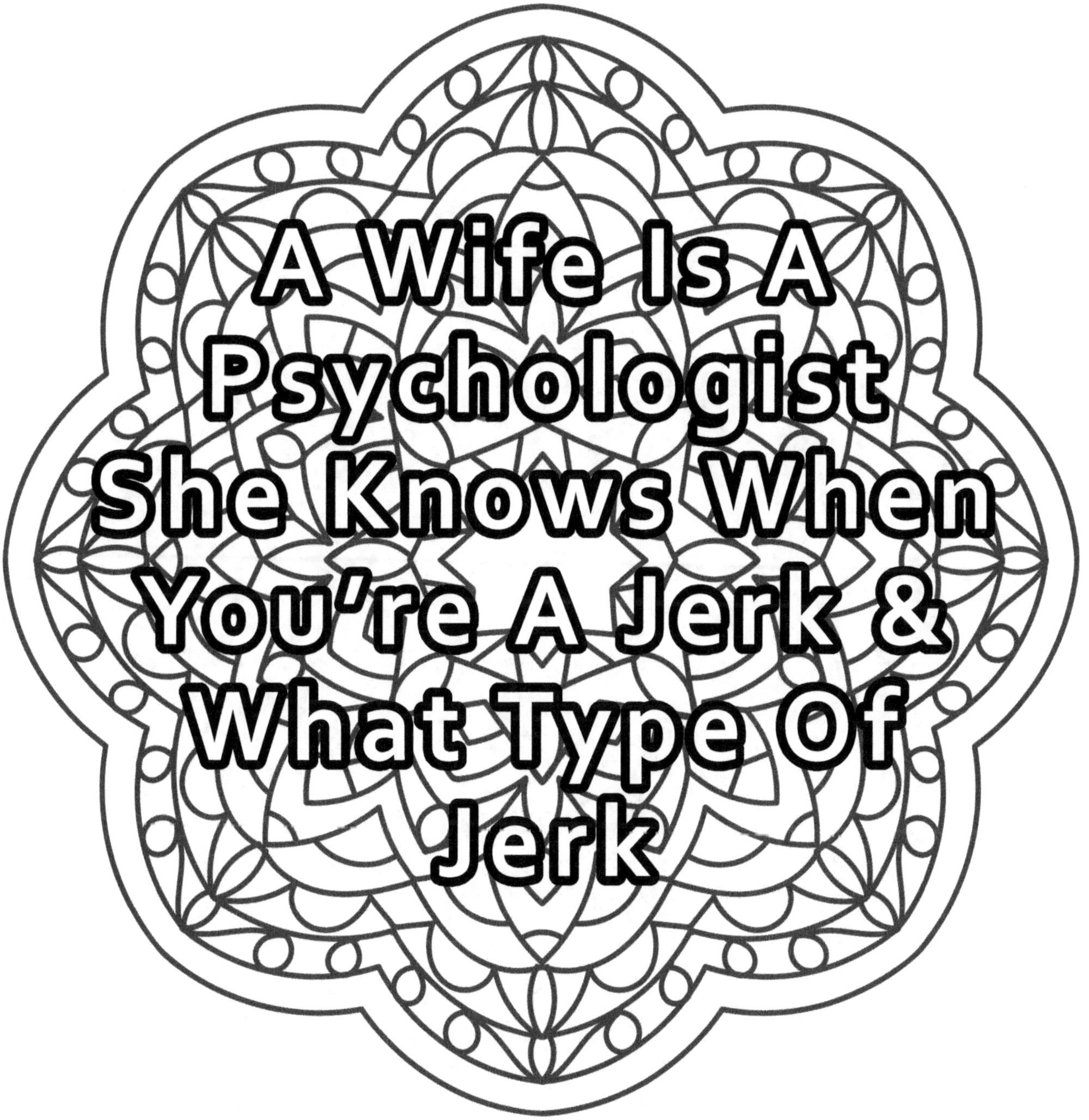
A Wife Is A
Psychologist
She Knows When
You're A Jerk &
What Type Of
Jerk

When A
Husband Gives
A Wife Flowers
For No Reason...
there is a
Reason!

A
Husbants
Most Brilliant
Achievement
Is His Ability To
get His Wife To
Marry
Him

Mrs
Always Right...
Mr
Never Right

Marriage
Lets You Annoy
One Special
Person For The
Rest Of
Your Life

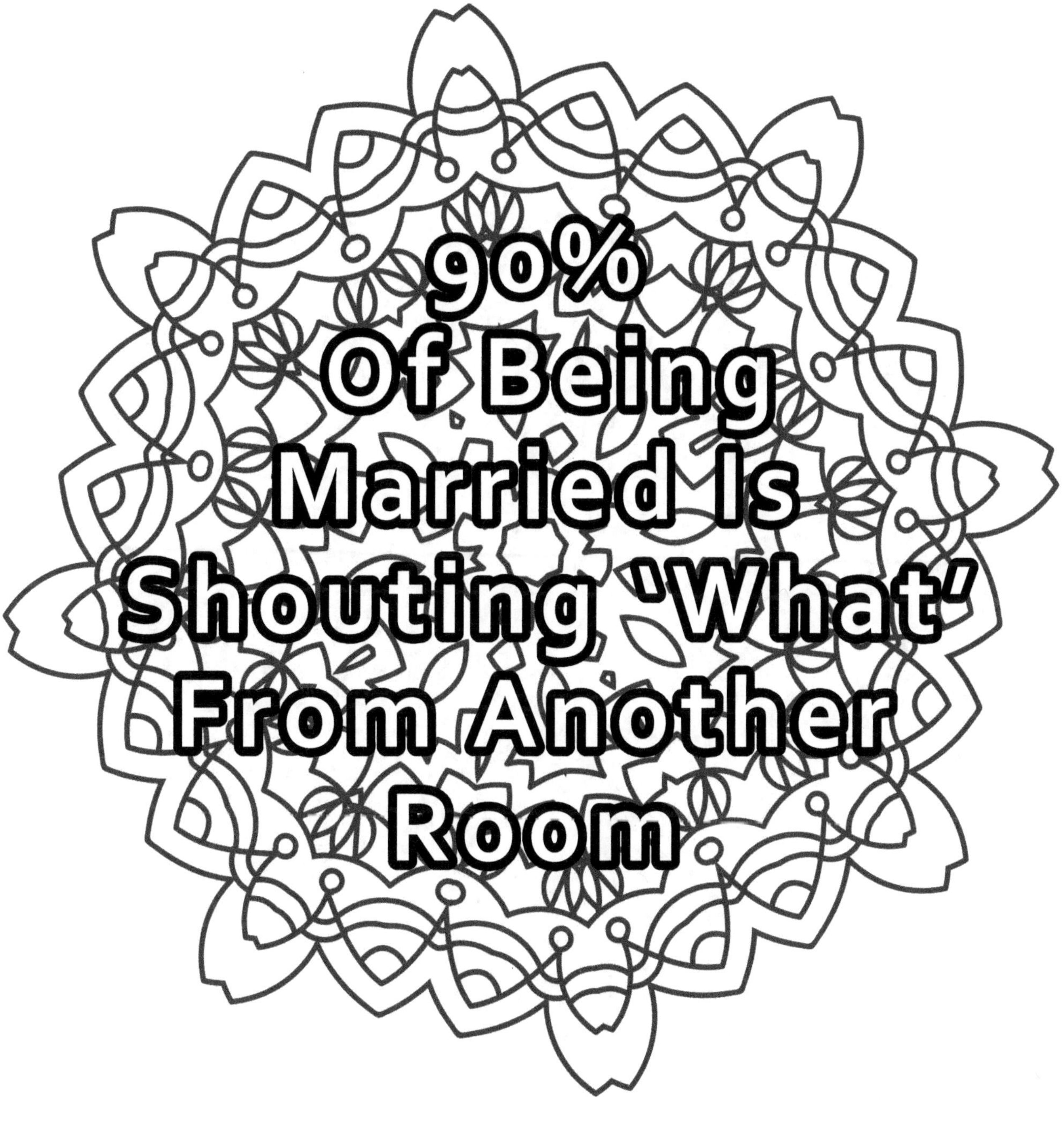
90%
Of Being
Married Is
Shouting 'What'
From Another
Room

Wedding Rings
Are The Worlds
Smallest
Handcuffs

I
Thought
I was Stupid
Before I Married...
After
My Stupidity Was
Confirmed

Tip
Your Wife Won’t Start An Argument With You If You Are Cleaning

COLOR TEST PAGE

www.ingramcontent.com/pod-product-compliance
Lightning Source LLC
Chambersburg PA
CBHW062127220526
45471CB00010B/3908